D0744242

arsico, Katie, 1980–
orking at a bank /

2009.   WITHDRAWN
3305217333875
06/04/09

21ˢᵗ Century Junior Library

WORKING AT A BANK

by Katie Marsico

CHERRY LAKE PUBLISHING * ANN ARBOR, MICHIGAN

Published in the United States of America by Cherry Lake Publishing
Ann Arbor, Michigan
www.cherrylakepublishing.com

Content Adviser: Sharon Castle, PhD, Associate Professor of Social Studies,
George Mason University, Fairfax, Virginia

Reading Consultant: Cecilia Minden-Cupp, PhD, Literacy Specialist and Author

Photo Credits: Cover and page 4, ©matka_Wariatka, used under license from Shutterstock, Inc.;
page 6, ©Daniel Dempster Photography/Alamy; cover and page 8, ©iStockphoto.com/jsmith;
page 10, ©Keith Dannemiller/Alamy; page 12, ©JUPITERIMAGES/Comstock Images/Alamy;
page 14, ©Corbis Premium RF/Alamy; cover and page 16, ©Rtimages, used under license from
Shutterstock, Inc.; cover and page 18, ©Steve Cukrov, used under license from Shutterstock, Inc.;
page 20, ©iStockphoto.com/JerryB7

Copyright ©2009 by Cherry Lake Publishing
All rights reserved. No part of this book may be reproduced or utilized in
any form or by any means without written permission from the publisher.

LIBRARY OF CONGRESS CATALOGING-IN-PUBLICATION DATA
Marsico, Katie, 1980–
 Working at a bank / by Katie Marsico.
   p. cm.
 Includes index.
 ISBN-13: 978-1-60279-270-8
 ISBN-10: 1-60279-270-4
 1. Banks and banking—Vocational guidance—Juvenile literature. 2. Bank
 employees—Juvenile literature. I. Title.
 HG1609.M27 2009
 332.1023—dc22   2008006768

Cherry Lake Publishing would like to acknowledge the work of
The Partnership for 21st Century Skills.
Please visit www.21stcenturyskills.org for more information.

CONTENTS

A bank is a good place to take the money you have saved.

What Is a Bank?

You are waiting in line with your **piggy bank**. It has taken you many weeks to save your money. It is time to put the money in a real bank. Now it is your turn to talk to the **teller**. She is one of many bank workers who can help you with your money.

Tellers help you make deposits into your account.

A bank is a safe place for your money.
Workers at the bank are there to help you.
Have you ever been inside a bank? Maybe
you even have your own **account** with
a bank.

Make a Guess!

Guess how much money tellers count every day. Write down your guess. Ask the teller for an exact number the next time you visit the bank. Was your guess correct?

Bank tellers must be good at counting money.

Tellers are just one example of workers who help bank **customers**. Many people do many different jobs in banks. They all work together to help you make the best choices about your money. Let's take a look at some bank workers.

A personal banker helps customers open bank accounts.

Bank Workers

You met the teller when you gave her your money. A teller helps you when you want to put money into your account. She also helps you to take money out of your account.

Not sure what to do with your money? A **personal banker** can tell you all the things a bank offers. He explains how the bank will help customers. He works with

A loan officer helps customers borrow money.

people who want to open accounts. Bank customers must often answer the personal banker's questions. They also sign papers.

Sometimes bank customers need to see a **loan officer**. This worker spends time with people who want to borrow money. She talks to them about how much money they need. She also explains how they will pay it back.

Most security guards wear uniforms. It is easy
to find them at a bank.

Who else works in a bank? Computer experts take care of a bank's computer system. **Accountants** and **lawyers** are important bank workers, too. They make sure banks follow special laws and do their best to help customers.

People take their money to banks to keep it safe. This is why banks have **security guards**. A security guard keeps people from stealing the money in the bank.

A bank manager is in charge of the bank.

Who is in charge of all the bank workers? A bank **manager** runs the bank. He hires many of the workers. You can talk to him if there is a problem with your account. The bank manager and his workers want you to be a happy customer!

Think!

Where do bank workers put all your money? Hint: Have you ever heard about a special room called a vault? A vault is where banks store money. The vault is always locked. Only certain bank workers are allowed to go inside the vault.

Bank workers need good math skills. They have to be able to count money.

Do You Want to Work in a Bank?

Would you like to work in a bank? You can start planning ahead right now! Talk to workers when you visit the bank. Find out what they needed to learn to do their jobs.

You may find out that many bank workers enjoy math. They need good math skills to count money.

Do you like keeping track of the money in your piggy bank? Maybe a job at a bank will be right for you.

Practice your math skills by counting the money in your piggy bank. Keep track of how much you put in and how much you take out.

A bank can be an exciting place to work. Learn as much as you can now. This is the best way to decide if one of the jobs you have just read about is right for you!

Ask Questions!

Bank workers are used to answering customers' questions. Why not ask them about their jobs? Find out what they do all day. Ask them what they like best about their jobs. Asking questions is one of the best ways to learn about jobs that interest you.

GLOSSARY

account (uh-KOUNT) money that customers put into a bank

accountants (uh-KOUN-tuhnts) people who are experts at managing money

customers (KUHSS-tum-uhrz) people who visit a business, such as a bank, to use a service or buy something

lawyers (LOI-urz) people who are trained to give advice about laws

loan officer (LONE AW-fiss-uhr) a worker who helps customers who want to borrow money from a bank

manager (MAH-ni-jer) a person who runs a bank or other business and is in charge of the other workers there

personal banker (PUR-suh-nuhl BANGK-ur) a worker who answers people's questions about products a bank offers and helps people open accounts

piggy bank (PIG-ee-BANGK) a container shaped like a pig that people keep money in

security guards (si-KYOOR-uh-tee GARDZ) a worker who protects a business, such as a bank, to make sure it stays safe for workers and customers

teller (TEH-lur) a worker who helps bank customers who want to put money into their account or take money out of it

FIND OUT MORE

BOOKS

Hall, Margaret. *Banks*. Chicago: Heinemann Library, 2008.

Klingel, Cynthia, and Robert B. Noyed. *Bank Tellers*. Minneapolis: Compass Point Books, 2003.

WEB SITES

Career Kids
www.careerkids.com/careers/index.html
Learn more about becoming a teller or bank manager

U.S. Department of Labor and U.S. Department of Education—Career Voyages
www.careervoyages.gov/students-elementary.cfm
Click on "Financial Services" to watch videos about different banking jobs

INDEX

ABOUT THE AUTHOR

Katie Marsico is the author of more than 30 children's books. She lives in Elmhurst, Illinois, with her husband and two children. She would especially like to thank the staff of Fifth Third Bank for helping her research this title.